This book is presented to:

_____

You are an awesome BYG
(Black Young Gifted)kid!

Illustrations by Blueberry Illustrations

Dear BYG (Black Young Gifted) Kid...

S. Laureen Brown

Copyright Registration Number: TXu 2-429-351
Effective Date of Registration: May 4, 2024

Library of Congress Control Number: 2024913605

ISBN: 979-8-9910678-0-5

Published by S. Laureen Brown
Contact information: slaureenbrown@icloud.com

Printed in the United States of America.

Acknowledgment

To God be the glory!

To all BYG (Black Young Gifted) kids,
this book is dedicated to you.
Never forget these
four simple but powerful words
as you go through life:

You Are Good Enough!

Dear BYG (Black Young Gifted) Kid,
Do you know how STUNNING you are?
Your radiant inner light shines as bright as the stars in the sky.
You are a beacon of hope for a better day.
You are Black, Young, Gifted, and AWESOME in every way!

Dear BYG (Black Young Gifted) Kid,
Do you know how UNIQUE you are?
Love the beautiful color of your skin because it sets you apart from the rest.
Embrace the distinct, natural texture of your beautiful hair.
You are often imitated, but can't be duplicated.
You are Black, Young, Gifted, and ONE OF A KIND!

Dear BYG (Black Young Gifted) Kid,
Do you know how INTELLIGENT you are?
You are capable of learning anything and achieving every goal that you set.
It's in your DNA! Nothing can stop you.
You are Black, Young, Gifted, and RESILIENT!

Dear BYG (Black Young Gifted) Kid,
Do you know how BLESSED you are?
By God's grace, you have rights and freedoms that our ancestors could only dream of.

Dear BYG (Black Young Gifted) Kid,
You will experience some things that others won't,
simply because of the distinguished, ancestral traits
that are the makings of you.
I pray that you will not be discouraged by the unjust
things that others do.

Never give up.
Keep dreaming.
Keep excelling.
Hold your head high.

You are loved.
You are good enough.
You are worthy.
You are special.
You are somebody.

In prayer, we will always keep you lifted.
May God bless and protect every kid, everywhere who
is Black, Young, and Gifted.

GLOSSARY

BYG: BLACK, YOUNG, GIFTED
STUNNING: Strikingly attractive or handsome.
UNIQUE: Being the only one of its kind.
RADIANT: Filled with love or happiness; glowing.
AWESOME*: Inspiring awe.
INTELLIGENT: Having or showing the ability to learn, think, understand and know.
DISTINCT: Not alike; different and separate.
CAPABLE: Having or showing the ability, power or strength needed for a particular activity or purpose.
RESILIENT**: Able to withstand or recover quickly from difficult conditions.
DISTINGUISHED*: Marked by eminence, distinction or excellence.
ANCESTRAL: Belonging to, or coming from an ancestor.
TRAIT: A quality that helps to set off one person or thing from another; characteristic.
FREE: Not controlled by another or others; Able to do, act or think as one wishes.
UNJUST*: Characterized by injustice; Unfair.

Note: Unless otherwise indicated by asterisks, definitions have been taken from The American Heritage Children's Dictionary,
© 1994 Houghton Mifflin Company.
*From www.merriam-webster.com(online dictionary).
**From www.google.com.

BYG (BLACK YOUNG GIFTED) KID
DAILY AFFIRMATIONS CHECKLIST

- ✓ I am BYG (Black Young Gifted).
- ✓ I am awesome.
- ✓ I am unique.
- ✓ I am intelligent.
- ✓ I am resilient.
- ✓ I am blessed.
- ✓ I am loved.
- ✓ I am beautiful.
- ✓ I am good enough.
- ✓ I am who God created me to be.
- ✓ I am all these things and so much more.
- ✓ I will work hard to make my dreams come true.

ABOUT THE AUTHOR

S. Laureen Brown is a Christian poet, author, entrepreneur, community advocate, and has been employed in the civil service sector of the local government for over 25 years. Her first book, Inspired Poetic Expressions: Christian Prayers and Poems, was released in 2021 and has blessed many readers.

Dear BYG (Black Young Gifted) Kid is her first children's book. The text for this book was originally used as a poem for a Black History Month program. Stephanie's goal is to promote and reinforce a positive self-image in every BYG (Black Young Gifted) kid around the globe who is given the opportunity to read this book.
In addition to writing, she loves gardening. She calls herself Sista Green Thumb because her small garden flourishes and produces a good harvest each year. Prayer, writing, and gardening are sources of peace and relaxation for her.

She recognizes that God has blessed her with the gift of encouragement through writing. She has written numerous encouraging poems for others. She will continue to encourage and inspire her readers with more uplifting books and poems in the future.

S. Laureen Brown can be reached via email(slaureenbrown@icloud.com) and on social media (@slaureenbrown on Facebook, TikTok, Instagram, YouTube, and Pinterest). Visit her online store at www.quiettimebooks.net to purchase her books and other great items.